NEW YORK YANKEES

DON WARD

CREATIVE EDUCATION

Reggie power. Yankee slugger Reggie Jackson (before he became an Angel) blasted dozens of homers out of Yankee Stadium.

Library of Congress Cataloging in Publication Data

Ward, Don, 1924-
  New York Yankees.

  Summary: A history of the Yankees from 1900 through 1981, highlighted by their twenty-two World Series championships and thirty-four American League pennants.
  1. New York Yankees (Baseball team) — History — Juvenile literature. [1. New York Yankees (Baseball team) — History. 2. Baseball — History] I. Title.
GV875.N4W37 1982   796.357'64'097471   82-12652
ISBN 0-87191-868-4

NEW YORK YANKEES

If you like baseball, you'll *love* the story of the amazing New York Yankees.

Since 1900, the fabulous Yanks have blasted their way through the pages of baseball history.

Over the years, millions of fascinated fans — people just like you and me — have thrilled to the booming home runs and brilliant fielding of the legendary Yankee stars.

In the Baseball Hall of Fame at Cooperstown, New York, you will find a golden list of baseball immortals who have worn the famous gray and white pinstriped uniform.

In the early days, it was guys like Babe Ruth, Lou Gehrig and "Joltin' Joe" DiMaggio who started the Yankees on their winning ways. Later on, it was men like Yogi Berra, Lefty Gomez, Mickey Mantle and Whitey Ford. And more recently it has been future Hall of Famers like Jim "Catfish" Hunter, Ron Guidry, Reggie Jackson, Graig Nettles and Dave Winfield who have carried on the Yankee tradition.

And what a proud tradition it has been! All in all, the Yankees have won twenty-two World Series championships and thirty-four American League pennants. The Yankees are the only team in history to win five World Series in a row (1949-1953), and also four in a row (1936-1939). Only two other teams have won three in a row even

The "Sultan of Swat" in a classic pose. Babe Ruth was unstoppable in his best years with the Yanks.

once — the Oakland A's (1972-1974) and the Chicago Cubs (1906-1908).

FAMOUS YANKEE RECORDS

It has been the Yankee players who have churned out some of baseball's biggest records:
* Babe Ruth's sixty home runs in 1927
* Joe DiMaggio's fifty-six-game hitting streak in 1941
* Roger Maris' sixty-one home runs in 1961
* Ron Guidry's 25-3 pitching record in 1978

Famous plays? The list goes on and on. In the third game of the 1932 World Series, the Yankee fans watched in wonder as Babe Ruth stepped to the plate and pointed to a spot in deep center field as if to say, "That's where I'm gonna hit the next pitch." Sure enough, a few seconds later the Babe delivered a mighty home run — one of the longest centerfield homers ever hit in Wrigley Field.

In 1953 at Washington's Griffith Stadium, Mickey Mantle surprised the Senators with a towering Yankee-style homer that sailed over the center-field fence and kept climbing and climbing until it was a tiny dot in the sky. Finally, the ball banged off a distant signboard high atop

The great DiMaggio gets a hit in the 56th (and final) game of the longest hitting streak in baseball history.

MAGIC 56
In 1941, DiMaggio hit safely in 56 straight games. In more than 40 years since then only Pete Rose has come anywhere near that record. Rose was stopped after 44 games in 1978.

the stands. Mantle had hit the ball almost 200 yards — a feat considered "impossible" until that day!

In 1978, the Yankee fans went wild again as Reggie Jackson treated them to another "impossible" feat. In the sixth game of the Yankee/Dodger World Series, Jackson smashed Burt Hooten's first pitch into the right-field stands for two runs. In his next time at bat, Jackson blasted Elias Sosa's first pitch into the right-field stands for two more runs. In this third time at bat, Jackson clobbered Charlie Hough's first pitch deep into the center-field bleachers for the final run in an 8-4 Yankee victory. Three pitches. Three home runs.

"Nothing can top this," Reggie shouted to reporters after the game. "I'm really happy for myself, but I'm also happy for the New York fans. They're the greatest fans on earth, and I thank God I came through for them."

It has always been this way. For the better part of an entire century, baseball fans from coast-to-coast have looked to the Yankees for action, excitement and surprises. It would take dozens of books like this to tell the complete history of the Yanks, but we will try to treat you to some of the real highlights in the next few pages.

The men you're about to meet have been selected from

The man who hit three home runs in one World Series game. Reggie Jackson was nicknamed "Mr. October" for his late-season Yankee fireworks.

an all-time roster of more than one thousand players who have worn the Yankee uniform over the years. In many ways, their story is the story of baseball itself. So let's begin at the beginning.

BASEBALL BEFORE THE YANKEES

It's hard to imagine, but professional baseball started more than 25 years before the first Yankee team was even formed. The very first pro team was actually the Cincinnati Red Stockings who toured the country soon after the Civil War.

In 1876, the National League was organized, but the game they played then was much different than today's version. Pitchers threw underhand. It took nine balls (rather than four) for a batter to get a base on balls. The distance from the mound to home plate was only 45 feet.

It was 1884 before pitchers were allowed to pitch overhand, and 1893 before the pitching distance was changed to the present 60 feet 6 inches. In those days, the players caught the ball barehanded. Wearing a glove was considered sissy stuff.

By the turn of the century, the rules had been changed to about the same as today's. In 1901, the American League was organized to compete alongside the National League

YANK FANS LOYAL
The Yankees have drawn over one million fans on the road for 35 years, including a Major League record 2,461,240 in 1980.

More than 75,000 fans jammed into Yankee Stadium to watch a duel between baseball immortals Babe Ruth and Walter Johnson.

teams. It would be two more years, however, before the first World Series would be played between the champs of both leagues. That same year, 1903, was the year the American League's New York Yankees got their start.

1903-1919
THE YANKEES BEFORE BABE RUTH

They were never much of a threat. Founded by Byron Bancroft Johnson (the first president of the American League), those early Yankees were more smoke than fire. For more than fifteen years, they struggled through long gloomy seasons — never winning a pennant, and seldom finishing above fourth.

In 1918, the frustrated Yankee owners coaxed Miller Huggins, the feisty little manager of the St. Louis Cardinals, to accept a new position as New York manager. Almost immediately, a new team took shape.

By 1919, Huggins had put together a solid hard-hitting infield, including four oldtime sluggers named Pipp, Pratt, Peckinpaugh and Baker. Together with outfield power-hitter Duffy Lewis and pitchers Ernie Shore and Bob Shawkey, the 1919 Yankees led the league in home runs, with forty-five.

Feisty manager Miller Huggins lured Babe Ruth to the Yankees in 1920. Huggins helped build a Yankee dynasty.

That same year, however, a lone Red Sox player by the name of Babe Ruth hit twenty-nine homers all by himself. Huggins made up his mind to lure the Babe away from the Red Sox to the Yankees. With the blessings of the Yankee owners, Huggins took the team wallet to California in 1920 to make the Babe an offer he couldn't refuse.

The Yankees promised Ruth a $1,000 cash bonus and a two-year contract at $20,000 a year. That may not sound like much compared to today's million-dollar contracts. But, in those days, a juicy hamburger cost less than a dime, and a shiny new car could be bought for a few hundred dollars. The Yankees had offered Ruth a salary that was four or five times larger than most big-league salaries at the time. When the Babe said yes, the first era of real Yankee power had officially begun.

THE SULTAN OF SWAT . . .

There has never been an American sports legend quite like George Herman Ruth. His picture-perfect swing and powerful personality colored all of baseball during the decade of the 1920s.

Though most Americans never had the chance to see Babe Ruth work his magic in person, they certainly saw his

Babe Ruth was jeered as an overweight has-been in 1932, but he proved he was still a king.

SULTAN OF SWAT Babe Ruth won the home run championship ten times in twelve years.

name and face in countless newspaper headlines, especially during the annual World Series. In those days, Babe Ruth was the king.

Born on February 6, 1895, George Ruth was the pride-and-joy of a friendly Baltimore saloonkeeper. As the years went by, however, Mr. Ruth found it impossible to keep his young son out of mischief. At age eight, George was brought by his parents to St. Mary's Industrial School for Boys, a very strict boarding school run by Xaverian Brothers. For the next ten years, St. Mary's would be his home.

The school had a rough, tough baseball tradition, and scrappy George Ruth fit right in. When he wasn't launching long home runs over the churchyard fence, he was out on the mound hurling sizzling fastballs and sliders. His reputation quickly spread beyond the walls of St. Mary's. In February, 1914, when he was barely nineteen, Ruth signed his first pro contract with Jack Dunn of the Baltimore Orioles, for $100 a month.

The veteran players at the Orioles' spring training camp took one look at Dunn's nervous young rookie and quickly nicknamed him "Dunn's babe." The name stuck. By the end of spring training everybody was calling him Babe Ruth.

The sweetest swing in baseball. Even the enormous power of Mickey Mantle couldn't help the Yanks in the dry spell of the late 1960's.

The Babe got his start in the major leagues as a left-handed pitcher for the Boston Red Sox. He was not a good pitcher, he was a *great* pitcher. By 1919, however, he had fallen in love with hitting. He convinced his coach to switch him to the outfield so he could play every game. He broke every home-run record in the books that year, sending baseball fans and excited sports reporters into a frenzy. But it was only a taste of greater things to come.

In the Babe's first year with the Yanks (1920), he clobbered fifty-four round-trippers out of the park. No other player in the league hit more than nineteen; no other *team* hit as many as the Babe did.

The next season, 1921, was even better. This time, Babe smashed 59 homers, drove in 170 runs, scored 177 and batted an astounding .378. Inspired by their moon-faced superstar, the Yankees won their first American League pennant and a shot at the awesome New York Giants in the World Series.

All in all, between 1921 and 1932, Babe Ruth's ferocious bat helped the Yankees win seven pennants and four world championships. More than any other, the 1927 season was a year the old-timers would never forget. This was the year the Babe hit a new record of 60 homers while leading his team to

ONE MEASLY RUN
Roger Maris topped Babe Ruth's season home-run record in 1961, smashing sixty-one round-trippers. In the Series, though, Maris batted a frigid .105 with one measly home run!

Roger Maris blasts his 60th homer of the season. He would hit one more in 1961 to break Babe Ruth's old record.

MURDERER'S ROW

The 1927 Yankees (Murderer's Row) — considered by many the greatest team in baseball history — went through the entire 154-game schedule that year using only 25 men.

110 victories and a shot at the Pirates in the World Series. The Pirates never had a chance. Like a giant steamroller, the Yanks flattened them out in four straight games.

When he wasn't playing baseball, Babe Ruth was usually out on the town. In many ways, the mischievous boy from Baltimore never really grew up. The Babe always had a special place in his heart for kids. He would make visits to the kids' wards at New York hospitals. He would stand for hours signing autographs. Once, after a tough mid-season game, the Babe found himself surrounded by a huge crowd of young fans. Instead of shooing them away, the Babe had the usher bring him a chair. It was long after dark when Babe Ruth had finished, but he had patiently signed his name for every kid in that crowd.

In some ways, Babe Ruth's last World Series produced his finest hour. The Babe was now aging fast and arguing with Yankee management. Lou Gehrig, not Babe Ruth, provided most of the fireworks in the 1932 Series, played against the Chicago Cubs. Sadly, Babe was jeered as an overweight has-been.

Then in the third game, with Cub fans howling insults at the fading star, Babe made that famous gesture. With two strikes on him, he pointed to the center-field bleachers and

Phil Rizzuto (center) pulls one of his patented double plays in this 1949 World Series victory over the Dodgers.

took a mighty whack. The bat connected and the ball went soaring for a home run — right to the place that Babe Ruth had pointed out. The crowd was strangely silent as the Babe trotted toward first. Then, finally, a deep roar of respect rose from the stands. The fans knew they had witnessed the Babe's finest hit. And it proved once and for all that he was the king of baseball, the "Sultan of Swat."

LOU GEHRIG,
THE STAR WHO PLAYED IN RUTH'S SHADOW

He was a pitcher and a slugger, as the Babe had been. But the Yankee scouts wanted him for his bat. Five years earlier, in 1920, he had earned a reputation as the best high school baseball player in New York City and, perhaps, the nation. His name was Lou Gehrig. His specialty was home runs. And his idol was the one and only Babe Ruth.

Gehrig was a powerfully-built 6-foot, 200-pound college sophomore when the Yankees offered him a contract near the end of the 1923 season. He was scared to death, but he accepted the offer and immediately found himself playing side-by-side with Ruth, his idol.

In thirteen games, young Gehrig batted an amazing .423 and walloped his first major-league homer. The Yan-

Mighty Lou Gehrig when he tied Everett Scott's record of 1,307 consecutive games played in 1933.

THE IRON HORSE
In thirty-four World Series games, Lou Gehrig drove in an incredible thirty-five runs. No wonder they called him the Iron Horse!

kees won the pennant by sixteen games. Babe Ruth finally had some competition in the batting department.

Except for their ability to hammer the baseball, Ruth and Gehrig had very little in common. Ruth was loud, tough and fun-loving. Gehrig was quiet, gentle and serious.

As the years wore on, Gehrig and the Babe avoided talking with each other. They played on the same team, but they did most of their talking with their bats. If Gehrig scored a home run, the Babe would try to answer with two.

In 1927, when the Yankees turned out their legendary "perfect season", Ruth batted .356 and Gehrig hit .373. The home-run battle between Ruth and Gehrig that year was the most exciting drama ever witnessed in baseball to that day. For the first time the Babe had a real superstar going homer to homer with him, attempting to whip the Sultan of Swat. On August 15, Gehrig was actually ahead of the Babe, thirty-eight homers to thirty-six.

By the end of the 1927 season, Gehrig and Ruth were first and second in the league in runs batted in. They were first and second in total bases, with 447 and 417. Gehrig led the league in doubles. Ruth led in bases on balls.

Home runs? Ruth had set a new record with sixty; Gehrig hit forty-seven. No other man other than Ruth had

Shortstop Tony Kubek was one of several legends playing for the Yanks in the 1964 World Series.

27

ever hit that many. The third highest home run total in the league was Tony Lazzeri's eighteen.

Today, many baseball fans still don't realize what a great player Gehrig really was. Sure, the Babe hit a few more homers, but Gehrig batted in more runs. While Babe got all the headlines, Gehrig played quietly and superbly in his shadow.

In 1939, the world was stunned with the news that Lou Gehrig, the pleasant Yankee star, was suffering from an incurable disease. On July 4, a Lou Gehrig Day was held at Yankee Stadium. Though Lou knew he would never play baseball again, he waved bravely to the crowd and told them, "All in all, I can say on this day that I consider myself the luckiest man on the face of the earth."

Babe Ruth was there in the park that day to hear those words. Quietly, the two batting kings hugged each other in front of thousands of saddened fans. It was the end of a great chapter in Yankee history. Two years later, Lou Gehrig lost his battle with his illness and died. But the memory of his great career is enshrined in the Baseball Hall of Fame — and in the hearts and minds of baseball fans throughout the world.

Yankee Shortstop Gil McDougald is upended while completing double play in 1956. Backing up McDougald was Yankee second baseman Billy Martin

TWO-MAN TEAM
In the 1928 Series, Ruth and Gehrig destroyed the Cardinals in four straight games. Ruth hit .625, highest of all Series batting averages, and Gehrig hit .545. The two sluggers batted in 14 runs between them, scored thirteen and had eleven extra-base hits (including seven home runs) in their sixteen hits.

THE GREAT DIMAGGIO
TAKES OVER

Famous sportswriter, Dave Anderson, says it best:

"During Joe DiMaggio's thirteen seasons from 1936 through 1951 . . . he batted .325 with 361 homers and 1,573 runs batted in. But the true measure of his importance to the Yankees is their success as a team — ten pennants and nine World Series championships in those thirteen years . . . Joe DiMaggio was the Yankees' star, baseball's star."

When Joe DiMaggio was a young boy, his father wanted him to be a helper on the family fishing boat. Joe gave it a try, but he was always getting seasick.

Joe's father was disappointed. He thought his fourth son was just lazy. When the older brothers were busy on the boat, Joe was usually off on the sandlots playing baseball with the neighbor kids.

Baseball — that's what young Joe DiMaggio lived for. At seventeen, he dropped out of San Francisco's Galileo High School to play shortstop for a local semipro team. He hit .633 that year. Suddenly, all eyes were on "Joltin' Joe."

At eighteen, Joe joined the San Francisco Seals, (a minor-league team) and went on a sixty-one game hitting streak. The lessons he learned setting that record would

Joltin' Joe DiMaggio slid past burly Ernie Lombardi to help beat Cincinnati in the 1939 World Series.

come in handy during a certain season with the Yankees, just a few years later.

The year was 1941. Joe DiMaggio was now the big bat for the Yanks who had called him up to the big leagues in 1935.

From 1936 through 1939, the Yankees had averaged over 100 wins a season. They had won four American League pennants, and four straight World Championships! Through it all, the great Joe DiMaggio had been the Yankees' inspiration. He was a flawless center-fielder. His arm was powerful and accurate. At the plate, he could do no wrong. The greatest pitchers feared him.

And then came 1941. One of the most amazing records in sports history began at Yankee Stadium on May 15 of that year. That was the day Joe DiMaggio hit a routine single against the White Sox. That little hit started a wave of excitement that would sweep over all of baseball during the next two months.

Day after day, game after game, the great DiMaggio would stretch out his string of hits. No one could stop him.

On June 29, Joe broke George Sisler's American League record of hitting safely in 41 straight games.

In July, he broke Willie Keeler's 1897 major-league record of 44 straight games.

Southpaw Whitey Ford sparked the Yankees in the '50s. Ford went on to win the Cy Young Award in 1961.

THE AMAZING GOOSE
Rich "Goose" Gossage, the amazing relief pitcher for the Yankees, always had a cannon for an arm. A good fastball sails over the plate at 90 mph. A great one might go 95 mph. But a Goose Gossage fastball whistles in at 99 mph — a little gray blur.

33

From games 47 through 56 he came to bat 40 times and connected for 23 hits, a .575 average!

Finally, on the night of July 17, 60,000 Cleveland fans watched as pitchers Al Smith and Jim Bagby, Jr. put an end to DiMaggio's streak. Still, Joe had hit safely in 56 straight games, leaving the number "56" as one of baseball's most glorious figures.

1949-1964
THE NEW YORK YANKEES BUILD A DYNASTY

It sounds impossible, but it's true. Between 1949 and 1964, the New York Yanks won 14 pennants and nine World Series crowns. It was, without a doubt, the wildest, craziest, most exciting 16 years in Yankee history.

Year after year, the New York fans sat hypnotized in mammoth Yankee Stadium as enemy teams were blown away by the guys at home. So many Yankee stars got their first chance to shine during this era that it's almost impossible to list them all here.

Even the Yankee managers were living legends. Casey Stengel managed the team to ten pennants in twelve years. Then came Ralph Houk who won three out of three. Finally, Yogi Berra won a pennant the one year he managed.

Casey Stengel chews out the umpire in 1949 action. Old Casey guided the Yanks to five Series titles, laughing and joking all the way.

How did they do it? They did it with guys like Joe Di-Maggio ... Mickey Mantle ... Whitey Ford ... Billy Martin ... Roger Maris ... Bobby Richardson ... Tony Kubek ... Phil Rizzuto and Gil McDougald.

They did it with Yankee style and Yankee pride. If you wore the Yankee pinstripes during this period, you were expected to uphold a "never-say-die" style of play. Yankees were supposed to be winners. And that was that.

In 1949, Joe DiMaggio — old reliable — paced the Yanks to a winning season that ended with a satisfying World Series triumph over the Dodgers.

This was the same year that a funny-looking old man named Casey Stengel came to New York to manage. Casey had a wrinkled little face, big ears, a pointy jaw, and a great sense of humor. When he had played for the Dodgers, Pirates and Giants back in the early part of the century, Casey had built a reputation as a rowdy outfielder with plenty of hustle. As a manger, he clowned around with everyone, including the players on the other team. But his sense of humor never interfered with his desire to field a winning team.

The Yanks loved old Casey. "Even when they lost, they had fun," explained a Boston sportswriter. But they sel-

Yankee first baseman Joe Pepitone (left) clutches his big 1964 contract, handed over by General Manager Ralph Houk.

WHAT ROOKIES! *Superstars Mickey Mantle and Willie Mays were both rookies in the 1951 World Series.*

dom lost. They weren't supposed to. They were Yankees.

In 1951, Stengel brought a 19-year-old rookie center-fielder to the Yankees. His name was Mickey Charles Mantle. The shy kid from Oklahoma could hit a ball as far as any man who ever lived. Mantle's first season was DiMaggio's last. Mickey did a good job of filling the Jolter's shoes. He hit a lifetime total of 536 home runs, including the 1953 monster homer in Washington that soared 565 feet. Like Babe Ruth, Mickey faced many pitchers who were afraid to throw the ball over the plate to him. They walked him instead.

Backing up Mantle and his bat was a squat little catcher by the name of Lawrence Peter "Yogi" Berra. Yogi was a smooth catcher and a big hitter. He was the Most Valuable Player in the American League in 1951, but most fans remembered him best for his funny way of talking. On Yogi Berra Night, he tipped his hat and said, "This is the best night I never had."

From 1950 to 1960, the Yankees won the pennant every year except '54 and '59. Out in the field were superstars like Phil Rizzuto, Gerry Coleman, Hank Bauer, Gene Woodling, Gil McDougald, Bill Skowron, Bobby Richardson, Tony Kubek and Elston Howard. On the mound the Yankees had powerful hurlers like Allie Reynolds, Vic Raschi, Eddie

Yogi Berra anchored the Yanks in this 1957 game against the Chicago White Sox. Twenty-five years later, Yogi would still be wearing Yankee pinstripes—as a coach.

Lopat, Bob Turley, Don Larsen, and the greatest Yankee pitcher in memory — ace left-hander Whitey Ford.

Billy Martin, who would manage the Yankees through three World Series in the late 70s, also sparked the Yanks at second during the 50s. Martin, who had problems controlling his temper, was better known as a troublemaker than a playmaker.

"Some people think Martin is a loser," said manager Stengel, "because he is scrawny and looks underfed. But he'll never let you down. Can he make double plays? Will he fight against big odds? Will he come through when coming through means most? You have to say 'yes' to all three questions."

The 1961 season was unforgettable. Yankee manager Ralph Houk became the third manager in history to win a World Series in his first year. Mickey Mantle knocked in 112 runs and ripped 54 home runs. But listen to this! Roger Maris, the Yankees' humble outfielder, chose this year to hit sixty-one homers. Maris' final home run of the year broke Babe Ruth's old record by one. Once again, a Yankee player had done what everyone else thought was "impossible."

Fiery Billy Martin, a former Yankee second baseman, came back as a manager to lead the team to greatness.

BILLY BALL
In the 1953 Series, Billy Martin batted a brilliant .500, banging a record twelve hits and eight RBI.

GEORGE STEINBRENNER AND THE MODERN YANKEES

In the 1964 World Series, the Yankees' Joe Pepitone hit a grand-slam home run to lift the Yanks to an 8-3 victory in game six. In the end, however, the St. Louis Cardinals defeated the Yanks for the World Championship. It was a sign of hard times ahead for the Yanks.

From 1965 through 1975, the Yankees tasted year after year of disappointing defeat. The worst year was 1966 when they wound up in the cellar. The old legends — Babe Ruth, Joe DiMaggio and Mickey Mantle — were gone. Sadly, there were no real superstars on the team to take their place.

When George Mitchell Steinbrenner bought the Yankees in 1972, he made up his mind to return the team to its winning ways — no matter how much money it might cost.

In 1974, Steinbrenner offered Jim "Catfish" Hunter a $3.35 million contract to come and pitch for the Yanks. Hunter, 28, had just won the Cy Young Award as the best pitcher in the American League. Still, baseball had never seen a contract offering so much money. Steinbrenner, of course, was just getting started.

By 1976, Steinbrenner had bought (or coaxed) a team of

Owner George Steinbrenner angered players, press and fans, but he restored the Yankees to a winning system in the late '70s and early '80s.

players who were finally able to make the World Series. Under fiery new manager Billy Martin, the Yanks fielded a powerful roster that included stars like Chris Chambliss ... Graig Nettles ... Lou Piniella ... Mickey Rivers ... Thurman Munson ... Sparky Lyle and Catfish Hunter. Though Cincinnati won the Series, the Yankees vowed to return the next year. They certainly kept their promise.

In 1977, superstar outfielder Reggie Jackson, joined the Yankees. It was history in the making. That year, the Yanks beat the young, talented Kansas City Royals to take the Amercian League pennant. In the Series, the Yankees took the Dodgers, 4-2. Jackson provided all the excitement anyone could ask for. He set a record for most home runs in a six-game Series. He belted five, including three in the final game at Yankee Stadium. Imagine, three home runs in a row! Only the mighty Babe Ruth had ever accomplished such a feat before. More importantly, the Yankees had won their first World Series championship since 1962.

In 1978, the Yankees were back in fine form again. This time it was Yankee pitcher Ron "Louisiana Lightning" Guidry who led the Yanks to another World Series victory.

Ron's statistics for 1978 were so special that he won the Cy Young Award as the American League's best pitcher by

Reggie fought with Steinbrenner and Billy Martin, but still found time to hit dozens of homers in the '79, '80 and '81 seasons.

REGGIE BARS
One night in Yankee Stadium, Reggie Jackson hit a key homer. From somewhere out of the crowd one of the excited fans threw a Reggie candy bar onto the field. Moments later, a torrent of the candy with the orange wrapper and the picture of the Yankees slugger cascaded out of the stands onto the field.

a unanimous vote. His regular-season record of 25-3 gave him a winning percentage of .893, the highest in history for a pitcher winning over twenty games. His nine shutouts were tops in the majors, and tied Babe Ruth's sixty-two-year-old league record for lefties. His 248 strikeouts broke a seventy-eight-year-old Yankee club record. Ron's courageous performance sparked the Yankees to their second World Series championship in a row — and earned a special page for him in baseball's most hallowed collection of records.

In 1979, the Yankees slipped to fourth, but they were back to finish first in 1980 and '81.

The '81 Series against the Dodgers has been called the most exciting World Championship in more than thirty years. Though the Yankees were ahead by two big games, the Dodgers battled back with four wins in a row.

Were the Yankees discouraged? "Not at all," said third-base veteran Graig Nettles. "The '81 Yankees were a great team, but the Dodgers must have wanted it a little more.

"One thing about the Yankees," Nettles smiled, "you know we'll come back and get you."

As he said those words, you could almost see Babe Ruth, Lou Gehrig, Joe DiMaggio and Mickey Mantle smiling, too.

Louisiana lightning. Ron Guidry and his awesome fastball led the league in strikeouts with 88 during 1980.

46

Graig Nettles was a machine at third base, as the Yankees powered to a 1981
World Series showdown with the Dodgers.

DATE DUE

LX NOV 1983	MAR 1 1 1987		
28 '83	Davie david		
L X APR 1984	JUL. 3 1987		
8 1984	BES DEC 1987		
FEB 1985			
1985	JUL 9 1988		
	APR 0 7 1989		
	APR 2 0 1990		

DEMCO 38-301